THE PERFECT COACH

A COACHES PERSPECTIVE

CHERYL DICKENS
& JULIE MATA

Table of Contents

Introduction

This book is a companion for coaches to utilize throughout their career. It was written by two softball coaches who have both coached at the High School and College level. We have been coaching a combined 26 years. We decided to write this book because we wanted to share our experiences with other coaches and guide them through the tough times that arise in sports programs. This understanding can only be learned through experience. So, utilize our knowledge and let this book be a guide as you continue on your path to success.

You are not alone in your chosen profession. Every coach has ups and downs in every season. These highs and lows could involve a player, parent, administrator, or even another coach. It's normal to feel overwhelmed at times, especially during season when you barely have time to sleep. Developing a program is no easy task. It involves loyalty from your coaching staff, discipline from your athletes, and support from your administrators and spouse.

What follows in the next chapters will help with situations you may face this season. To begin, everything has to be executed on both the coach and the player's side. The coaches have to implement, organize, and enforce discipline. The athletes have to execute, buy into your program, and get along (at least on the field) with the other players. A big difference between male and female athletes is that females are typically more sensitive and they usually care what their coaches and other players think of them. They often carry outside troubles onto the field and at times have less self-confidence and motivation. It is your job as the coach to communicate with your athletes, care about their lives (in regards to school and athletics), and get them to perform at the top of their talent level. They not only need to excel in practice, but also on the field or in the gym by using whatever creative ways you can.

This book will give you an idea of what types of players you have on your team, as well as the parents you inherit, whether you want to or not.

Remember during those tough days that you aren't alone and for every bad experience or player there are so many more positive ones. You should focus on those moments and let the negative ones roll off your back. If you don't, you will likely burn out fast and there won't be

enough happy hours to make you truly happy.

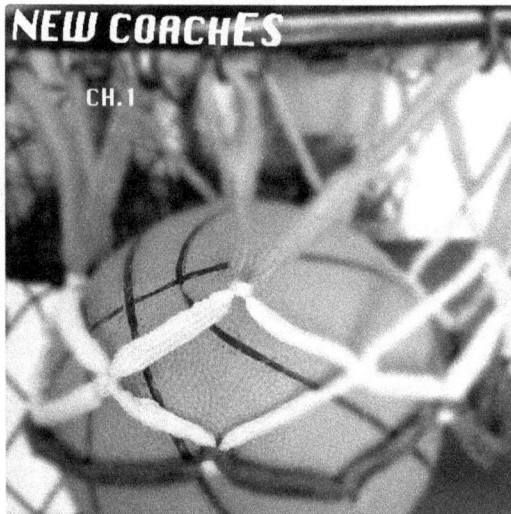

NEW COACHES

CH.1

A good place to start (if you haven't already) is to find out what the team had success with last year in regards to fundamentals, practices, players, and strength of schedule. After all you aren't re-inventing the wheel. A good source for this information would be your AD, assistant coach or former players. It would also benefit you to watch pickup games or research about your team from the past two years. If you're going into a program that is having a hard time getting wins then you may have to do a complete overhaul. If that's not the case, then subtle implementation of your strategies and ideas should maintain an already successful team. The worst thing you could do to the morale of a winning team would be to change everything that the players feel made them successful. Female athletes don't like too much change at one time.

After you know more about the program you've taken over, the next step is to introduce yourself to the athletes. Opening the line of communication will take some edge off the awkward first impressions. There will inevitably be some staring and wondering what kind of coach you are for your first meeting. If you don't do this step then the players won't know what to expect from their new coach and may have negative feelings because of the coaching change. Let the players know your philosophies early on and where the team is heading. By doing this you will show them leadership, trust, and respect, three of the most important traits of a healthy and successful coach and team.

During the off-season, begin with discipline and remember to follow through. You have already gone over your rules so this is your first chance to define your team. If someone is late or if someone isn't going all the way through the line you need to do something about it. The team is watching to see if you mean what you say. Treat all players equally, from your best players to your second string. This will keep the team happy and save you a conversation about having "favorites." At the beginning of your season stay in a routine until the players start to understand how you coach and what you expect. Once they buy into your way of coaching then change things up and keep them on their toes. Always have high expectations for your team and they will work harder. Incorporate conditioning, weights and team building to bring the players closer together. Also, during the off-season create team goals and make sure that your team chooses most of them, as they will be more likely to follow the goals that they have set.

Discuss with them the need to hold each other accountable for their intensity during practice and execution of plays on the field or court. There will be several conversations outside of practice that you will never hear about (or want to). It is important that you have team leaders that believe in your goals for the program to be your voice outside of practice. When you have strong leaders, the negative players seem to weed themselves out.

ch. 2

The 21st Century Athlete

I know that I sound old, but I find a noticeable difference in this generation of student-athletes. It seems that more parents do the talking for their child athletes, often acting like agents when it comes to recruiting, and players are not as responsible for their actions or for themselves because of this. It also seems they are less likely to set realistic and specific goals for themselves, either in academics or athletics. They complain more about classes. Again, I know I sound cranky, but I want more women in our country to realize it wasn't that long ago when they couldn't vote... and there are still countries in this world today (Afghanistan!) that don't allow girls to get more than a primary education, that makes griping about 8:00 a.m. class seem silly, doesn't it?

When I sat and thought about the difference in today's athlete, it came down to a plethora of excuses. Why do so many of them find explanations instead of finding solutions, answers, a better work ethic, and more successful results? I can't understand why players would rather coast in classes and get Bs and Cs instead of working for As.

When did it stop being cool to sit in the front row, doing it right, and striving to get the best grade possible? I'm starting my own revolution to get young women to WAKE UP! I don't think it's just my team that is accepting the B-C mediocrity in the world today. My opinion is that if they are mediocre off the field, they are probably going to be mediocre on the field as well. When things get hard in a game, they will probably revert to coasting mode. When it's hard to communicate, they will probably just pout and keep to themselves.

Making excuses *never* involves finding a solution or a better way. It is merely a way to explain your failure to someone who wonders why you failed. Excuses are often less for others to hear and more for one's own ego. It's how we justify failure to ourselves rather than taking that long, hard road to fixing the problem or improving.

Another thing I see in today's athletes is the way they walk and talk and act around others. In our society it has been proven time and again that when people are in groups, they tend to act unwise. They are less likely to help someone in need, and more likely to talk loud and do things with less inhibition than they would likely do on their own. When I go to tournaments to recruit, I rarely, if ever, wear my university logo on my clothes. I like to see how kids are going to act during games and in between games. A trade secret: I like to sit in the middle of a group of parents and get the story on the team and players by listening in on their conversations. It *never* fails that either in between games, or at the hotel restaurant for breakfast, or in a restaurant near the fields, I'll see players in groups being loud, rude and offensive. They wouldn't act that way if the family sitting next to them were their own. They wouldn't use the kind of language some of them use today (and quite loudly, I might add) if they knew a college coach was sitting next to them rather than a lady reading a book or sitting with her husband and son. I've noticed group/team behaviors growing far worse over the last few years than anything I encountered in my first decade of coaching.

What happened to the athletes who do whatever it takes to get on the field or court?

When I played we won and lost together as a *team*. Now, there are three types of athletes that make up the dynamic of a team. You have the lazy players, Pre-Madonna's and scrappy players.

You will recognize the "lazy players" in your first conditioning work out. These are the girls who will be the first to say, "I Can't!" They will be the first to drop out of a workout because it's too hot, they can't breathe, or they have a pain in one of their extremities, which are a few of the many excuses I've heard over the years. I shouldn't say that they wouldn't do whatever it takes, because they will do whatever it takes to get out of a workout. If they put as much time in their practices as they do trying to get out of it, they would possibly become one of the better players on the team.

The "Pre-Madonna" players are the good players but will never be great. They are unpredictable and won't reach their full potential because they won't let themselves. These players have too many travel coaches and "know" they know more than you! Also, when you talk in the huddles, they will be looking into the stands because really, what could you possibly say that they don't already know? Besides, if there were anyone to blame for a loss, it would be someone other than them. Their parents have praised and convinced them that they can do no wrong. The frustrating thing is that these players are usually the leaders and have the strongest influence and voice on the team. You can only hope they lead the team in the right direction.

The "scrappy players" are the athletes who would be at the top of an All-Star list of all current and former players. These athletes may not fundamentally be the best, but they would do "whatever it takes". They buy into your philosophy, work the hardest in practice, lead by example, love the game, and are loyal to you.

Scrappy players create their own luck. They make the ESPN plays look easy because they go all out. Some of these players have little natural talent but have a big heart and will push their teammates. The others in this group will end up being the stars of your team. These players are the biggest reason we as coaches come back every season.

Team Building
Ch.3

When I started coaching in college, I was naïve enough to believe that any player that listened to my coaching philosophy during the recruiting process and chose to play for me would display all of the following traits: love for the team, passion for the game, loyalty, pride in performance as a student and as an athlete, and integrity. I quickly learned that just because players tell you they believe what you believe and that they see the same vision you see, they wouldn't necessarily make it happen. In the real world, as Alan Jackson sings, it's not that easy at all.

So, the question that I find most important to address when building a team is, "Who is a fake team player and who is for real?" When I was a kid I watched a lot of *Leave it to Beaver* re-runs on television and there was a young character named Eddie Haskell that was a trouble-making friend of Beaver's older brother, Wally. Eddie was a jerk, but anytime Beaver and Wally's parents were around he'd say something like, "My, Mrs. Cleaver, you sure look lovely today." He'd have that broad, fake grin on his face and pretend to be the perfect kid, all the while being an instigator of trouble behind the scenes. As a coach, it's clear to me that one of the biggest problems when building a team is weeding out the Eddie Haskell; and my theory is that this job gets harder the older I get. Let me explain...

When I had just turned 26, after three years of coaching high school athletics, I became the head coach of a University softball team that was in only its second year of existence. Being young and in charge has its own set of difficulties in coaching, but one of the best benefits you can get from it is that you can relate to the players so well. You are closer to where they are in regard to their thoughts, dreams, problems, and lives in general. As you get older, and the team stays the

23

same age, you eventually come to realize that you've lost touch with some of their thoughts, feelings and beliefs. The challenge then becomes finding common ground. When it comes to finding potential Eddie Haskells, find the players on your team that love the game and learn to get them to speak up, weed out the problems, and be the eyes and ears for you.

I'm not talking about players becoming "rats," "moles," "stool pigeons," or any other disloyal-sounding animal, for the head coach. I'm talking about perfecting the art of deciphering who is truly with you as a coach and with your program as a team player, and being able to read their looks, mannerisms, etc. that point out which player or players on the team are faking the positivity to the coach.

Sometimes your solid players, your "gamers" as many people call them, will just tell you that there is a problem with someone. It has been my experience, however, over the last handful of years that fewer and fewer players feel comfortable doing this. In fact, in the two years of coaching in which I consider my teams to have under-achieved; I learned that there were numerous players that were violating rules. For example, Player A couldn't tell on Player B for violating the drinking policy because Player B could tell on Player A for violating the attendance policy. In other words, the pots couldn't call the kettles black. This is why, when I talk about following team rules, I stress following *all* of them, because when players don't do so just once, they have to accept others not doing so for the long haul. It is also why, in retrospect, I see how crucial it is to find a strong core of players who truly believe in my coaching philosophy and are willing to speak up for it, to me, or to their teammates when I'm not around.

As a coach, I need to be able to see when my gamers look a little put out with a player or players in practice, on a road trip, or in a team meeting. Usually, it gives me a heads up that someone isn't acting the way she should.

I have started talking to my team at the beginning of the year about the gardener and the garden analogy. As a coach now in my early 40s, I can relate to this, and I think my players can understand this when I relate it to them and our team in general. It goes like this:

The team is the garden; the head coach is the gardener. When the garden is first planted (start of the year), every plant is treated the same by the gardener. Some plants (returners/upperclassmen) have stronger roots and have grown more in the garden than others and have produced more. As time goes on, some weeds (problem athletes) start to sprout around the plants. The gardener has a big garden to tend, so she doesn't always see the weeds sprouting right away. She can see the weeds when they get big, but when they first arise, the plants right next to the weeds can see them right away because they are on the same level. Productive plants don't have weeds around them. When weeds get big enough, sometimes they get out of hand and the gardener has to pull them, and a few bad plants along with them! My message to the team is if you see a weed, point it out. Weed out your own problems if you care about your team and your teammates. If, as a player, you don't want to see a teammate kicked off the team for breaking a team policy, stay on eye-level with your teammates, especially the new ones. Don't let things like alcohol, bad attitudes, and other bad influences affect your productivity.

As a coach who is now officially old enough to be the mom of some of my players, I realize that I miss more weeds than I used to. I have to work harder to get my eyes on "ground level" to see the problems that are around my players. I have to trust that my core group of gamers is going to lead and at times be my eyes for me. To build a strong and successful team, my core group of players has to really get it. They have to believe in my philosophy and me, otherwise--as I've seen with two underachieving teams in my 16 years at the college level—it doesn't matter how much talent they have.

TEAM SUCCESS
ch.4

I have broken a teams' success into a simple formula: Discipline + Team + Confidence = Success. I have coached teams with one or two of these key ingredients and they have all fallen short of their goals. With this formula of success beginning with discipline, your team will go farther than skills could ever take them.

The first step, discipline, is just as important as teaching athletes the fundamentals of the game. Your team will be tougher on the playing field or court, and mentally and physically stronger. The main thing to remember with discipline is to say what you mean and mean what you say. If you want your athletes to run through the line then they have to run past the line with no excuses or they start over. It is possible for a team to win some games without discipline but the wins won't feel as monumental and losses will drag the team down. Without strong discipline the wheels will eventually fall off and the chances are, luck won't be on your side. Discipline is the glue that binds a team together.

The next part of the formula is team. When your athletes work hard and believe in each other there will be more weight taken off of your shoulders. They will hold each other accountable and the girls that play only for themselves will stand out like sore thumbs. They will weed themselves out and make your decisions more evident. Showing teammates what they have in common outside of your sport will allow them to invest in one another. Team building will bond your players, strengthen their relationships and will help define your team.

The final step will be to make your team feel and become confident. You will need to implement practices and conditioning workouts that are challenging but also possible to complete successfully. Your players have to know individually and as a team that they can succeed in every situation they face.

These steps begin in the off-season. Athletes need to be pushed passed their limits to see what their thresholds are and also be given the confidence that lets them know they can do anything.

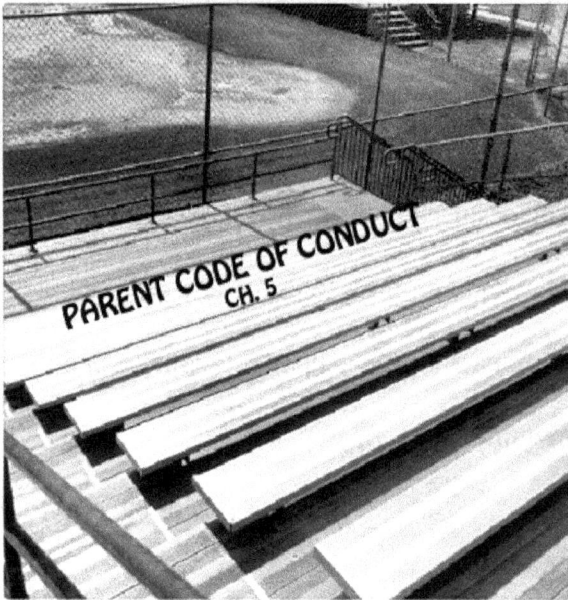

PARENT CODE OF CONDUCT
CH. 5

Working with and knowing how to communicate with parents on all levels is crucial to success, despite when it becomes difficult to not become angry and want to shut them out. I've done that before and realize that it's a mistake. At the same time, I have a theory called "I-can-balance-my-checkbook-so-I-could-be-anaccountant." It basically follows the ridiculousness of someone like me thinking that just because I know how to balance my checkbook (parents have coached little league or ASA) that I could walk into an accounting firm (coaches office) and tell the executive (head coach) how to do his or her job! Ridiculous, but so many parents think that just because they coached a bit or played slow-pitch (your sport) that they know more than you! Parents can be the best part of your program or the worst. The hard part is that you can't make everyone happy. The only thing you can do is be fair, give chances at practice for improvement, be direct with the athletes and care about them. If you do this you will make 98 percent of everyone happy. The other two percent that make you re-think your job every year are the parents that don't watch practices and think you are doing their daughter a disservice by not playing her. You will never please these parents or daughters, and it's because of this 2 percent that you need to make sure you document situations. You will be able to pick out these parents quickly. Make sure to document anything that comes to them or their daughters because they will do anything to get you fired if it comes down to it.

Make sure that during one of your meetings at the beginning of the season you discuss the expectations that you have regarding the behavior of your parents and athletes. If one of the two has a problem about playing time, the athlete needs to talk to you first. Most complaints can be resolved with communication between you and the athlete regarding what they need to do to get more playing time. If the parent still wants to meet, make sure your assistant coach is in the room as well as the athlete and parents. That way there is no hearsay and there is open communication with everyone involved. After you have documented this meeting the matter should be over. Be sure to have a 24-hour cooling off rule in place. This rule states that for the 24 hours before or after a game, neither a player nor parent can discuss any issues with you. This allows them to cool off if they are upset and think more logically before talking to you. Most of the time the situation will have worked itself out and you won't even hear about the issue. This rule also allows you to make decisions based on what's best for your team without any intimidation or outside factors. It keeps the game fair for the players and allows you to do your job as a coach. Parents' are a great asset to any team as long as they understand and respect your boundaries.

As a coach, one of your many hats (whether you want it to be or not) is to be the complaint department for players, and parents, who've felt you've wronged them. I feel that this should be a caveat at the end of every coach's contract. You will be there to listen to all complaints about you and your program, or to be closure for a player or parent who is left with a bitter taste in their mouth at the end of the season. When they are done venting the only professional thing you can say is, "Thank you for bringing that to my attention, I will take it into consideration." Don't ever get into an argument with a parent or athlete. If they have a problem and have come to you it's because they are upset with something you have or have not done and it is affecting them in some manner. The reason we document is to have facts. So when someone is upset, you will have the facts to back up your decisions. The best advice I have ever been given was when I was at a clinic in Georgia. Sherri Coale said, "not to roll with pigs" referring to anyone who likes to get dirty when they have confrontations. They get a thrill out of calling you out and just want to see a reaction from you. They are like pigs, don't get in the mud "you'll get dirty and they'll like it."

Be advised that every season there will be one or two players or parents who will not be happy with your decisions reflecting the athlete's playing time throughout the season. They may not agree, but you make your decisions based on what's best for the team. There are three perspectives you should consider to help your communication with the team: your perspective, which is focused on the team; the player's perspective, which is focused on their playtime; and the parent's perspective, which is what they see from the stands. Just understand that for every two negative players there are at least eight girls who appreciate what you do. These coachable players who play outside the box will be the only reason you stick around some years. Coaching is a difficult position to be in because there are so many aspects to it, but the positive changes you make in these girls lives in the end is the greatest feeling in the world.

HIGH SCHOOL COACH CH. 7

As a high school coach you will quickly learn that without the community and all stakeholder you will have a difficult time running your program. You can't do it alone and having support will help improve your job security, because more people will see how much effort you put in. High school parents want to be involved as much as you will allow them. You might have to put your foot down with some parents or they will try and run all over you. For example, I have heard stories of a coach at a new school where the parents worked on the field for her, sat in the stands at practice, and made strong suggestions on where the fundraising money should be spent. You have to have a balance, where the parents feel a sense of ownership but also know their boundaries. You ultimately have the say and it needs to remain that way or you will not have a voice in your own program. Be cautious of this and start the year off with your parent meeting organized and direct. Have parents volunteer for the jobs you need done throughout the season such as parent rep, concession stand workers, fundraising committee, or ticket takers at home games. It is also important that you recognize them as much as possible for the help they provide and communicate your appreciation of their efforts.

During your first meeting discuss your holiday game schedule to make sure the parents and players understand your policies. You may think that your players know that they are expected to be at every game, but from experience, I know this is not true for all athletes, especially around holiday time for the non-starters. Their parents may have already booked a trip; you will need to be prepared for this to happen at least once every year. There will be some conflict in schedules and you will need to know how you will respond. If you let one player miss games or practices for vacation then you can't tell another player next year that it's not okay to miss for the same reason. Also, be aware of which athletes play other sports or who are in a University Interscholastic League sponsored event such as band or choir that conflicts with your sports schedule. Decide how to handle each situation before the season begins. This will save you a lot of stress and off the cuff decision-making.

As a high school coach you are a teacher first and a coach second, even though the hourly breakdown of time spent on the field or in the gym will make you feel like the opposite is true. As well as the fact that most coaches received their position because of their coaching abilities. You get paid so much more as a teacher. Make sure you take care of your responsibilities in this area. Here is a hint: make your principal and athletic director very happy! Give them team shirts to wear at your games every year, and don't forget about the secretaries and the maintenance workers. This goes a long way when you need something done on your field, in your gym or in the classroom, like when you need your class covered at the last minute.

When you schedule games, review what the team's schedule has been in the past. The coaches of those teams will usually already have you listed as playing each other, and if they are a good team this is an easy way to fill your schedule with quality games. Another big thing is to be cautious of setting up games around the holiday breaks. You won't be able to get around having a game over a holiday, but you can be mindful of giving the players (and parents) a few days off to have family time. (This shows your priorities on family values as well.) A happy team provides more athletes, volunteers for the concession stand, press box, and ticket takers. Maybe even a bonus at the end of the season.

There are several certifications you need to make sure you get before your season starts. Most schools are requiring a Commercial Drivers License to drive the bus (which includes a three day class and yearly physical), first aid and CPR certification, and yearly online trainings such as concussion testing, sports rules testing, steroid and drugs review, etc. Do not be a procrastinator on these. It's a hassle, but complete them early so you can have less to do right before your season.

The biggest thing to remember as a high school coach is that not all of your players want to or will play in college. You will need to balance your practices by incorporating a sense of toughness and competition for the college-bound athletes, and an atmosphere of fun for those who just want to be a part of something. This is one of the harder challenges as a high school coach. At most schools you need enough players to fill two teams. If you are lucky enough to have so many you have to cut players, then make your team the way you want. You don't have the extra pressure of worrying about numbers. Plan to share your athletes with other sports. Most athletes will choose to play one sport by their junior year, but the really talented athletes will play more than one sport and you will need to compromise with the other coach to get that athlete prepared for your season. Another issue is sharing the weight room with all of the other sports. Make sure you have a scheduled time for your team to be in the weight room or the larger teams may kick you out. A good rule of thumb is to have the in-season sports lift after school (because they can) and the off-season sports lift during the athletic period.

High school is about sharing your athletes, the school's equipment, your assistant coaches and your time. Learn to get along with everyone, but don't give up what your team needs to be successful. Don't be a "yes man." Choose your battles wisely. Always promote your sport. Visit the middle schools to encourage interest. Invite these students to your games and have annual free clinics for them. This will incite enthusiasm for your sport and program. The younger players will feel invested in your program and look forward to

playing for you from an early age.

COLLEGE COACH
CH. 8

As a college coach, many people will tell

you this is a business and you should act

accordingly. To me, if you buy into that, you are

doing it wrong. In fact, I've proven a handful of

times now in my own almost two decades worth

of coaching, that the opposite is true, when I've

approached my job as a business, I've failed dramatically!

To do it right, remember that this is about the journey. This is about your players. It's you and them and the atmosphere for their parents. It's the success at the end of the day, the week, the month, the semester, and season. But it's mostly about what kind of people they turn out to be. It's about what they remember about it all 10, 20, 30-some years down the road.

This is about relationships through team building, challenges, and competition. This is about bringing out the best in people. Your job is to bring your own personality into the mix, be true to who you are, and *lead*. If you want to lead the right way, I believe you have to stop trying to be like other coaches you see just because they may experience the number of wins you'd like to have. *Instead* capitalize on how to communicate the way you know how with your own strengths. You can certainly borrow things you like from other coaches that you admire, but blend those techniques into who you are and how you coach. Coach because you love to bring out the best in people.

Your administration might define your job in black and white terms. You might be told that you are expected to win a specific number of games. It is my experience that most administrators will not want to hear you say that W's aren't your concern. So, I keep that little tidbit of information to myself, but I know in my heart that the scoreboard at the field doesn't tell the story. Don't forget *why* you are coaching.

Define it for yourself and then make sure to communicate it to your team if you want to thrive.

The least successful years I have had in my career have been when I have lost my way and tried to keep up with the Jones's at such and such university up the road! W's will take care of themselves when you stay true to your beliefs in how to succeed your way. You need to establish to your team *your* clear philosophy on what success is. You need to have those core beliefs solidly embedded in your team from year to year. In doing so, a strong nucleus of player-leaders will always be reinforcing them to the new players who come into the program each year.

The best part of your job is coaching on the field or in the gym. In fact, leading your players and your staff is the exciting part that most of us sign up for. You don't always consider the "other duties as assigned." You will probably also work on your field or court (few softball coaches have socks or shoes that aren't dirt and grass stained!), likely be the scheduling director, arrange your travel, act as chief fundraiser, drive a bus/van on occasion, lead community service efforts, and, of course, you will recruit, recruit, recruit.

In regard to fieldwork, I see numerous junior college, NCAA and NAIA softball coaches dealing with their own fields or court setup. From what I see, few NCAA Division II (my division for 17 years now) coaches have field maintenance crews. As I've aged, I realize that I have to get more and more help from my assistant coach and volunteer coaches who are looking for experience, but I still find myself preparing the field for games and helping with field prep before practice. If you go into a job "green" in this area, I suggest checking with other coaches in your league or go to a field maintenance crew to get some hands-on pointers.

When I started coaching, I wasn't the norm; I was never an assistant prior to head coaching, and I'd never had my own field to tend. I was 26 and I had inherited a second-year college program with a new field. Some of the weeds on my infield were taller than me. Unfortunately, the baseball coach who "helped" me learn the ropes seemed to enjoy showing my failures and watching me do things the hard way. If I had it to do over again, I'd call a few other programs in my league and visit them to see what their field maintenance schedules entailed. Most college coaches these days initially have great mentors from which to learn, plus the internet can help you learn. While there are no quick fixes to getting this part of the job done, there are definitely easier ways to do things. My advice in this area is to work on it daily, keep a regular schedule, and then the little tasks never become the big ugly tasks. For example: edge the infield and broom your edges daily; this will be a quick chore that will prevent you from doing a huge chore later!

A last note on fieldwork: do *not* make your players do it all. College athletes in other sports aren't dust mopping their courts, picking up bleacher trash after their football game, watering their field down after the fourth quarter, etc. Treat your college softball athletes like they matter! You might have one small task assigned to each after a practice or game, but if they are doing everything and you are sitting on a bucket or gator and driving in circles, don't expect them to levy a great deal of respect your way.

Scheduling is time consuming as a college coach. Unlike high school scheduling, college coaches are generally required to get game contracts drawn up with opponents for home contests. This is basically used to guarantee that teams will show up, barring unforeseen emergencies or bad weather. Probably the biggest job in scheduling is getting the tournaments you want. You have to keep in mind that you primarily need to play in-region, non-conference opponents prior to the beginning of your conference schedule. College coaches like to get the tournaments we wish to attend for the upcoming season locked in prior to June (you generally have three to five weekends to work with). If you don't get this taken care of early, you usually struggle trying to find a great location. Unfortunately, most college softball budgets don't cover tournament play, which usually requires extensive travel.

Travel arrangements are typically another time-consuming duty that a coach must take on in the college. I have to turn in bid requests for charter buses and get requests for van rentals depending on how far our trips will be. This varies among universities, but you do still see some of us driving the 15-passenger vans (we take three of these when we drive ourselves) on road trips. We don't have to get bus certifications, yet we do have to take driver's safety courses. Hotel arrangements can be tedious, so my goal is to get a quality, well-known chain hotel that might be a few extra dollars than the norm, but will assure safety, cleanliness and no hassles. I do these tasks early in the fall semester so I can share the information with our friends and families and they can make arrangements to stay where we stay if possible.

Handling your budget is an issue that college coaches definitely have to stay on top of. Although most athletic departments establish their own policies, the universal truth for us all is be a good steward of how you use your money. My coaching mentor told me that messing up in this area is the fastest way to lose your job.

Community service is another job that I've had to learn to balance. I find specific services that are different from those that other programs are doing in my community. We try to mow yards for people who can't mow their own. We collect used clothes and eyeglasses. We collect Boxtops for Education and donate them to local elementary schools. There are so many ways to give, and I try to pick ways that will challenge my team and be rewarding for them as well.

Recruiting for your sport is a beast all its own. While there are elements of it that I truly love, there are some things that have become a bit ridiculous, most of which stem from how some college coaches treat the process. I once heard a collegiate coach say it is "all one big cattle auction." To him, it's clearly a business. In my view, it is about finding young women that will match up with your university, your program and your coaching style. Finding fundamentally sound players is easy. Finding the heart and soul that will plug in nicely to your program is the key. When college coaches act like players are "cattle" and they make "bids" on them, it causes the whole ugly relationship in which some parents and team liaisons act like sports agents. I catch some slack for not wearing all of my university apparel when I recruit, but I really enjoy watching players I'm interested in from an incognito point of view. This is how I find my best players.

In addition to coaching at my university, I also teach. I teach two classes per semester and I truly enjoy it. Not all coaches like to teach, but it reminds me of the lesson cycle I created, which is a great method to use when coaching a practice as well. It goes something like this: Tell 'em what you're gonna tell 'em, have a focus, tell 'em what you need to tell 'em, check for understanding, practice, evaluate, re-teach if mastery isn't obtained, review, and close with something exciting for tomorrow!

As a coach, there are plenty of moments that aren't the "thrill of victory." To prevent the burnout and disappointment that occasionally tries to creep in, establish a strong group of peer relationships for support, ideas, and humor, humor, humor. Smile. I've found it beneficial to send out a weekly newsletter to my team, their parents and family, any friends of the program and/or alumni that are interested, and even some recruits that are interested. This is a great way to show the weekly progress of the team and establish a strong family relationship for our program. It's also fun for me to put my voice and opinions out there for all to read. If you want to be a great leader for a college team, you have to learn to communicate. I learn more about it everyday.

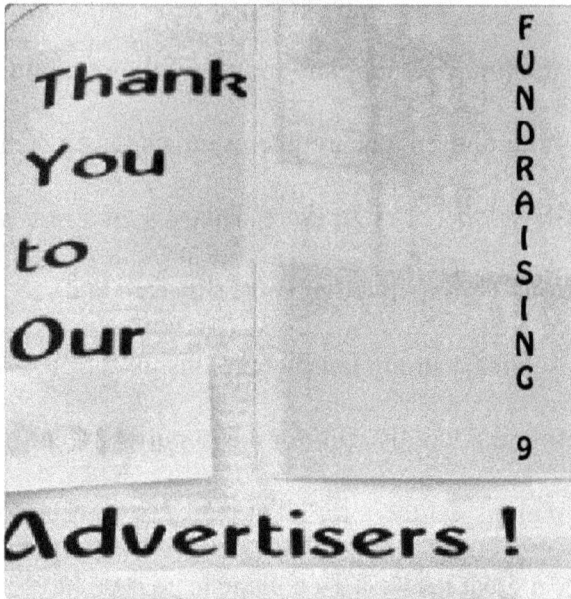

Thank You to Our Advertisers !

FUNDRAISING 9

For High School's you will need to talk to the AD about additional funding for your program. Your PTA should have a set amount of money for each sport. Be advised that if you are asking them for an item that cannot be passed down from year to year to your players (such as socks) the PTA will probably not give you money for it. The items that most coaches ask for include: practice clothes, uniforms, bags, sweats and equipment. Another important thing to be aware of is that the more of your parents who donate money and become members of the PTA, the more likely your bigger items will get approved. During the PTA meetings, they might review the percent of parents from each sport who are members and it looks bad if you comprise only 20 percent and another sport comprises 50 percent. So, get your parents involved.

When you fundraise you want to create an event that will get the community interested, excited, and one that people will want to donate to and attend. The other thing that will make your program more money is word of mouth and advertising for your event spoken by your players. Fundraising is not something you can make mandatory for your players, so you need to explain to them what fundraising does for them specifically. One idea that has been successful for me in the past was hosting an all-star game. Your team sells the ads for the program and they keep the money plus whatever you make from the concession stand. You will need to form a committee and delegate jobs to the people with the best knack for the job. You can also put together a golf tournament; this takes a lot of time to organize but is well worth it. If you want to go smaller, you can do car washes on the weekend or have penny-by-the-foot contests and have the girls get sponsors who will pay a penny a foot for how far the ball is kicked, hit, etc. This is typically a lot more fun for the athletes than running an event.

Whatever you decide to do, as a coach you will need to be an advocate to your parents, players and the community about volunteering because you can't do it alone. Get your ideas approved by your AD and be aware of the regulations your school has in place for fundraising. They may want you to ask only the businesses on your school's vendor list, or limit you to one fundraiser a year. It's always important to have a plan before inquiring about your school's policies.

At the University level fundraising can be a nightmare if you aren't at a school that knows how to do it right. I'm at a university in which we have a huge booster club and the corporate sponsors from our surrounding community are plentiful. This is a blessing. It helps fund the scholarship program at our university. However, since each individual program can't go around asking its corporate members for more than they give the department in general, my task becomes establishing fundraisers in the fall that will help boost my budget. We generally do letter writing campaigns, hit up our alumni, have hitting contests, etc. We work concession stands and we've also been known to sell a sno-cone or two. Fundraising isn't fun, but in an age of economic issues and seeing programs being cut left and right, you should make every effort to do it and show you are doing your part not to put a financial strain on your university.

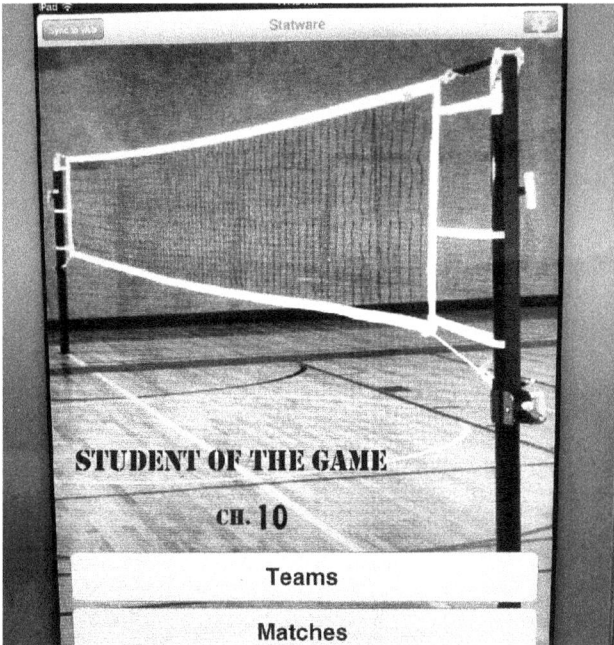

STUDENT OF THE GAME
CH. 10

To keep up with the changes in your sport you should attend at least two coaching clinics a year. Go to ones that you are interested in and you know will help you with what you need to work on as a coach. These clinics will not only give you tips for the upcoming season but also revitalize and remind you why you love coaching.

Once you feel like you know everything there is to know about your sport, you should stop coaching. There are so many ways to teach fundamentals, manage your team, and organize your program. Learn from your peers. Even if you only get two new drills from your trip it is worth it. If you stay on one track too long you will get in a rut that will be difficult for you to see and climb out of. The game changes and you must be adaptable to technology and the needs of your athletes in the changing years, or the game will leave you behind.

The Perfect Coach

- Only correct players who want correcting when they want to be corrected.
- Play all players an equal amount of time.
- Let all parents give input on coaching decisions.
- Make *everyone* happy.
- Don't let your feelings get hurt; coaches aren't supposed to have feelings.
- Don't get irritated when your team isn't focused or playing up to its potential; just realize the team will probably work it all out for themselves in time.
- Allow players to make up the rules and only follow them when it's convenient.
- Never be over or under aggressive in your offensive or defensive strategies.
- Never *ever* say one team you've coached over the years is better than another team you've coached, because it will hurt someone's feelings, and everyone will be happier if you pretend they're all equal.
- When a player's parents get angry with you, sit down and visit with them about what you can do to better please them. After all, the parents are indeed the number one priority.
- Don't expect to be treated the way you treat others.

- Bend over backwards to help players get scholarships, find jobs, fill out resumes, etc., but don't expect them to remember it once they are on their own, unless they need your help again.
- When there is a tough decision to be made about cutting a player, don't forget to explain everything in detail to your team so they can let you know if they agree or not.
- Look the other way when a player doesn't feel like working hard.
- Look the other way when a player sets a bad example of what your program is supposed to be about.
- Give most of your scholarship money to the most important position player, but don't expect more effort from them.
- If a parent calls and tells you her kid is bipolar, and that this is why she is causing so many problems, don't be caught off guard if the same parent calls your athletic director and tries to get you fired for agreeing with her.
- If players want to put derogatory pictures and statements on a web site that would misrepresent your program, don't let it bother you; just be content that they hide what is in the pictures and in the statements from *you* most of the time. It's not "misrepresenting" the program if they're representing who they *really are,* right?

- Don't care about players' personal lives; let them make mistakes often and freely, without passing judgment.
- When players finish their eligibility, always remember them fondly and speak highly of them, but don't expect the same in return.
- If players underachieve, tell them it's okay.
- Make sure you invite all players, even the bitter ones, to your alumni games. They won't come to the game, but they'll be even angrier with you if you don't send the invitation.
- Take your low-paying job seriously, but don't expect all parents and players to view it with any respect. After all, parents and players could easily do what you do better than you do it, but just chose not to coach because the job doesn't pay enough, and coaches get no respect.
-
- *Note: Please send any derogatory remarks or disagreements to my dad. I'm 40 years old, but since I'm a former athlete, my parents fight all my battles and deal with any unpleasant things for me.*

"The difference between a successful person and others is not a lack of strength, not a lack of knowledge, but rather a lack of will."—Vince Lombardi

THE PERFECT

COACH

"The only place where success comes before work is in the dictionary." -Billy Martin

"TALENT WITHOUT DISCIPLINE IS LIKE AN OCTOPUS ON ROLLER SKATES. YOU HAVE A LOT OF MOVEMENT, BUT YOU DON'T KNOW WHICH DIRECTION YOU WILL GO"-H. Jackson Brown, Jr.

"YOU CAN'T GET MUCH DONE IN LIFE IF YOU ONLY WORK ON THE DAYS WHEN YOU FEEL GOOD." -NOLAN RYAN

Conclusion

I hope that reading that last chapter put a smile on your face and made you realize we are not alone in our experiences. As a coach, you can't win all of your battles. There is no such thing as a perfect coach, because you can't play everyone on the team all the time, even though it causes ill fillings among some of your players. I had this epiphany after going to a coach's clinic: every coach needs help. No one knows it all and the sooner I grasped this the easier it was for me to focus on where I wanted my program to go, and the happier I became as a coach.

So here are my final words of advice. You get what you put into it. You may never be appreciated or liked, but coaching isn't about that; it is about believing in the coach that you know you are. You have to keep working on your areas of weakness and strengthening them by getting an assistant who is strong where you are not, or going to coaching clinics and learning from your peers. Some coaches get lucky enough to have been given great athletes or to have recruited great athletes. But a successful program is having everyone on your team believe that they are the best and being able to perform that way. It's about developing productive, self-confident athletes with good character. Don't be discouraged if they don't all buy into what you are trying to do for them. It takes some of them years to understand that it's not all about the wins on the scoreboard or about them; it's about putting the best group of athletes together with one common goal, believing in each other and their coaches. When this is accomplished, you truly are the Perfect Coach.

Connect with me online:
Facebook.com/theperfectcoach

www.ingramcontent.com/pod-product-compliance
Lightning Source LLC
Chambersburg PA
CBHW051045030426
42339CB00006B/203